i hate war, but i hate our enemies even more
arranged by heath schultz 2016
designed by becky nasadowski 2018
isbn 978-1-57027-360-5

released in collaboration with minor compositions 2019
colchester / new york / port watson

minor compositions is a series of interventions & provocations
drawing from autonomous politics, avant-garde aesthetics,
and the revolutions of everyday life.

minor compositions is an imprint of autonomedia
www.minorcompositions.info | minorcompositions@gmail.com

distributed by autonomedia
po box 568 williamsburgh station
brooklyn, ny 11211

www.autonomedia.org | info@autonomedia.org

[arranged by heath schultz]

i hate war, i hate our enemies even more

designed by becky nasadowski

a critical theory of the spectacle cannot be true unless it joins forces with the practical movement of negation within society. this negation—a reinvigoration of a revolutionary struggle—equally requires a critique of the spectacle. critique must be immanent to the spectacle, embodying negations' destructive possibilities. such a theory expects no miracle from the oppressed.

it views the reformulation and satisfaction of proletarian demands—liberation through the destruction of the whole social capitalist order—as a long term undertaking. the creation and communication of a critical theory cannot be imagined outside of a rigorous practice—the arduous path of theory must also be the path of the generalized resistance to capitalism and spectacle.

with writing came a consciousness no longer conveyed and transmitted solely within the immediate relationships of the living— an impersonal memory that was the memory of the administration of society. "writings are the thoughts of the state, and archives are its memory."

to articulate the past historically does not mean to recognize it "the way it really was." it means to seize hold of a memory as it flashes up at a moment of danger. historical materialism wishes to retain the image of the past which *unexpectedly appears to man singled out by history at a moment of danger. the danger affects both the content and the tradition of its receivers. the same threat hangs over both: that of becoming a tool of the ruling classes. in every era the attempt must be made anew to wrest tradition away from a conformism that is about to overpower it. only that historian will have the gift of fanning the spark of hope in the past who is firmly convinced that even the dead will not be safe from the enemy if he wins. and this enemy has not ceased to be victorious.*

> can a society part with, and triumph over, the very plunder that made it possible?

watts man: **I say this much as a human being that has been misused: Would you have something to fear from me if you attacked me? Answer it yourself, would you have something to fear from me if you attacked me?**

reporter: **You would use bloodshed?**

watts man: **No one knows what I will do. But would you fear? You don't know how I would respond? No one knows, like I told you. But that reaction is what you must fear.**

reporter: **Burning?**
watts man: **No telling.**
reporter: **Looting?**
watts man: **No telling.**
reporter: **Blood?**
watts man: **No telling.**

How can I explain something that another man may do? I'm only human and I can only see myself and I can't see that much of myself because I am only human and no one knows a man's mind. I don't even know my own mind. I don't know what limits are set on me. You don't either. That is why you fear. That is why I fear.

This is what we'll have to look at.

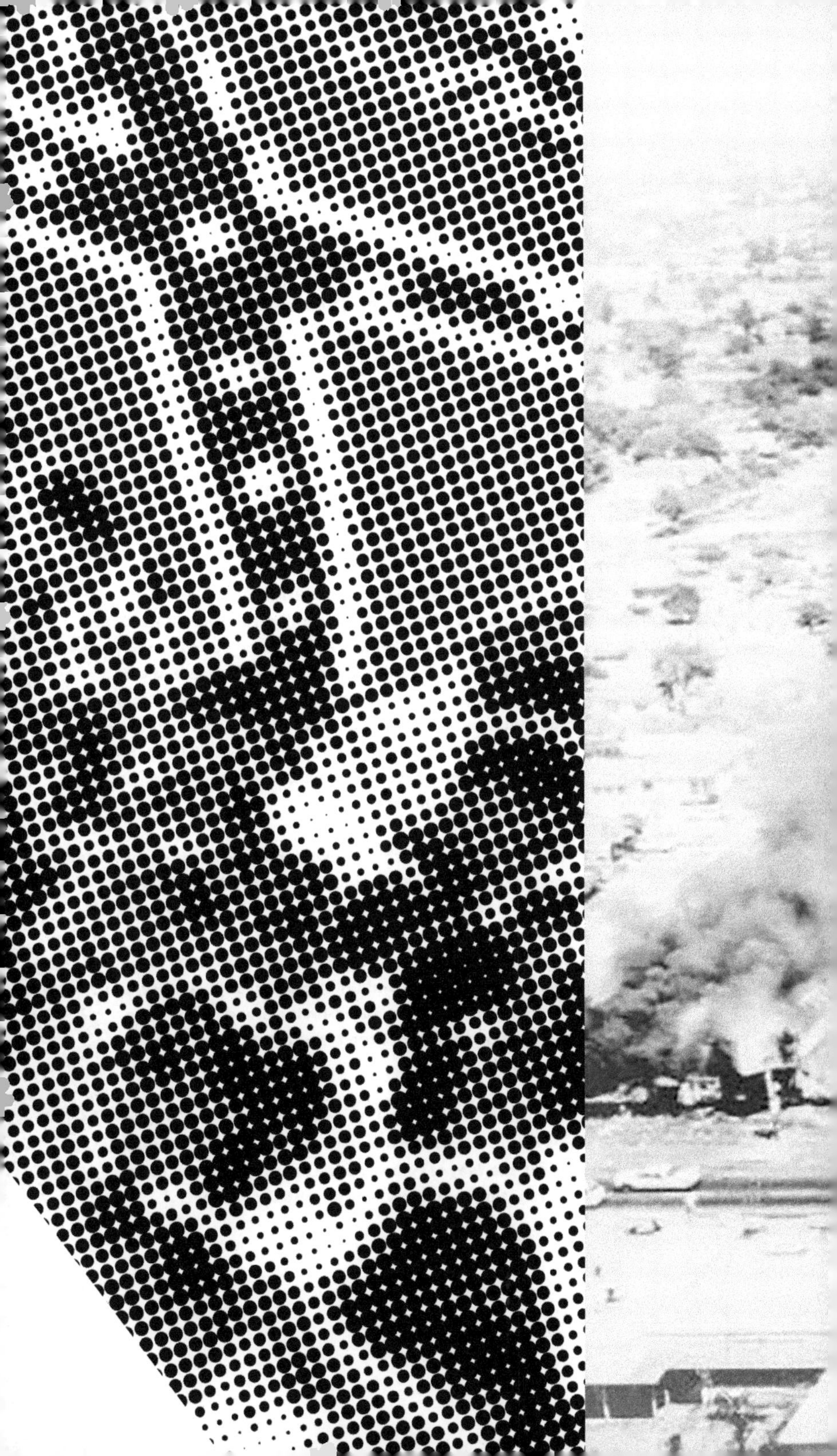

The philosophers Camus and Sartre raise the question of whether or not a man can condemn himself. The black existentialist philosopher who is pragmatic, Frantz Fanon, answered the question. He said that man could not. We in SNCC tend to agree with Fanon—a man cannot condemn himself. If he did, he would then have to inflict punishment upon himself. An example is the Nazis. Any of the Nazi prisoners who, after he was caught and incarcerated, admitted that he killed all people he killed, had to commit suicide. The only ones able to stay alive were the ones who never admitted that they committed a crime against people. There's another, more recent example provided by the officials and the population—the white population—of Neshoba County, Mississippi. They could not condemn Sheriff Rainey, his deputies, and the other fourteen men who killed three human beings. They could not because they elected Mr. Rainey to do precisely what he did; and condemning him would be condemning themselves.

In a much larger view, SNCC says that white America cannot condemn herself for her criminal acts against black America. So black people have done it—you stand condemned.

This is the day of my Inauguration as Governor of the State of Alabama. And on this day I feel a deep obligation to renew my pledges, my covenants with you—the people of this great state. General Robert E. Lee said that "duty" is the most sublime word in the English language and I have come, increasingly, to realize what he meant. I shall do my duty to you, God helping, to every man, to every woman, yes, to every child in this state.

Today I have stood, where once Jefferson Davis stood, and took an oath to my people. It is very appropriate then that from this Cradle of the Confederacy, this very Heart of the Great Anglo-Saxon Southland, that today we sound the drum for freedom as have our generations of forebears before us done, time and time again through history. Let us rise to the call of freedom-loving blood that is in us and send our answer to the tyranny that clanks its chains upon the South.

In the name of the greatest people that have ever trod this earth, I draw the line in the dust and toss the gauntlet before the feet of tyranny and I say: segregation now, segregation tomorrow, and segregation forever.

Watts, 1965

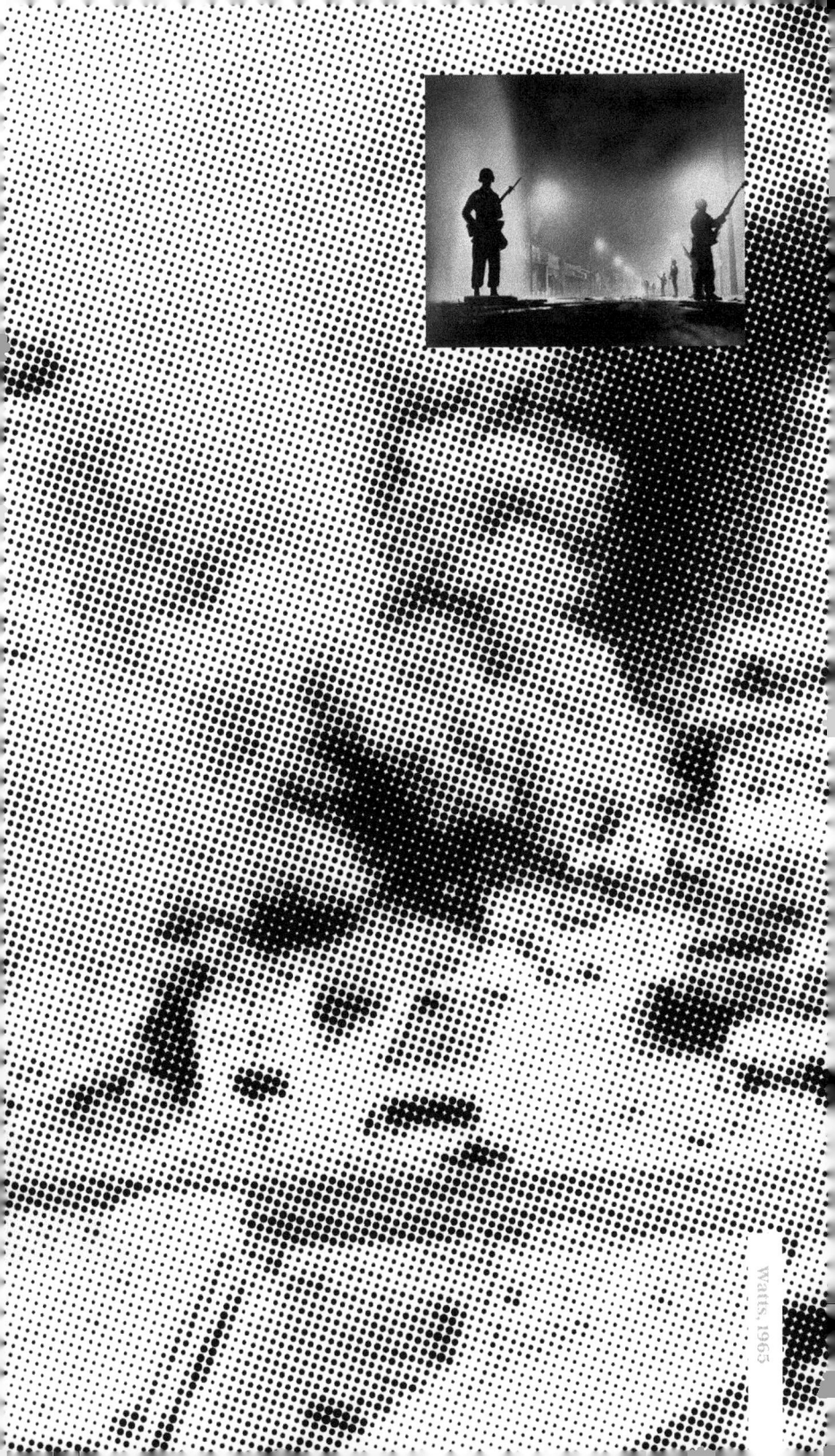

The institutions that function in this country are clearly racist; they're built upon racism. The questions to be dealt with then are: how can black people inside this country move? How can white people who say they're not part of those institutions begin to move?

Several people have been upset because we've said that integration was irrelevant when initiated by blacks, and that in fact it was an insidious subterfuge for the maintenance of white supremacy. In the past six years or so, this country has been feeding us a "thalidomide drug of integration," and some negroes have been walking down a dream street talking about sitting next to white people. We didn't go to Mississippi to sit next to the Governor, we did not go to Selma to sit next to the Sheriff, we went to get them out of our way. In order to understand white supremacy we must dismiss the fallacious notion that white people can give anybody his freedom. A man is born free. You may enslave a man after he is born free, and that is in fact what this country does. The only thing white people can do is stop denying black people their freedom.

Let us send this message back to Washington by our representatives who are with us today—that from this day we are standing up, and the heel of tyranny does not fit the neck of an upright man... that we intend to take the offensive and carry our fight for freedom across the nation, wielding the balance of power we know we possess in the Southland... that we will determine in the next election who shall sit in the White House of these United States... That from this day, from this hour, from this minute, we give the word of a race of honor that we will tolerate their boot in our face no longer.

To realize our ambitions and to bring to fruition our dreams, we must take cognizance of the world about us. We must re-define our heritage, re-school our thoughts in the lessons our forefathers knew so well, first hand, in order to function and to grow and to prosper. We can no longer hide our head in the sand and tell ourselves that the ideology of our free fathers is not being attacked and is not being threatened by another idea, for it is. It is an idea of government that encourages our fears and destroys our faith—for where there is faith, there is no fear.

I am black. I know that. I also know that while I am black I am a human being; therefore I have the right to go into any public place. White people don't know that. Every time I tried to go into a public place they stopped me. So some boys had to write a bill to tell that white man, "He's a human being; don't stop him." That bill was for the white man, not for me. I knew I could vote all the time and that it wasn't a privilege but my right. Every time I tried I was shot, killed or jailed, beaten or economically deprived. So somebody had to write a bill to tell white people, "When a black man comes to vote, don't bother him." That bill was for white people. The failure of the civil rights bill is due to the white's incapacity to deal with their own problems inside their own communities.

We are now engaged in a psychological struggle in this country about whether or not black people have the right to use the words they want to use without white people giving their sanction. We maintain the use of the words Black Power—let them address themselves to that. We are not going to wait for white people to sanction Black Power.

Where there is fear, there is no faith. It is an ideology of government erected on the encouragement of fear and fails to recognize the basic law of our fathers that governments do not produce wealth. People produce wealth—free people. Its psuedo-liberal spokesmen and some Harvard advocates have never examined the logic of its substitution of what it calls "human rights" for individual rights, for its propaganda play on words has appeal for the unthinking.

Not so long ago men stood in marvel and awe at the cities, the buildings, the schools, and the autobahns that the government of Hitler's Germany had built—just as centuries before they stood in wonder of Rome's building. But it could not stand, for the system that built it had rotted the souls of the builders and in turn rotted the foundation of what God meant that men should be. Today that same system on an international scale is sweeping the world. It is the "changing world" of which we are told. It is called "new" and "liberal." It is as old as the oldest dictator. It is degenerate and decadent.

9

As the national racism of Hitler's Germany persecuted a national minority to the whim of a national majority, so the international racism of the liberals seek to persecute the international white minority to the whim of the international colored majority so that we are footballed about according to the favor of the Afro-Asian bloc. But the Belgian survivors of the Congo cannot present their case to a war crimes Commission, nor the Portuguese of Angola, nor the survivors of Castro, nor the citizens of Oxford, Mississippi.

It is this theory of international power politic that led a group of men on the Supreme Court to briefly bare the ungodly core of communistic philosophy in forbidding little school children to say a prayer. It is the spirit of power thirst that led the same President to launch a full offensive of twenty-five thousand troops against a university—in his own country and against his own people. We have witnessed such acts of "might makes right" over the world as men yielded to the temptation to play God... but we have never before witnessed it in America. We reject such acts as free men. We do not defy, for there is nothing to defy. As free men we do not recognize any government's right to give or deny freedom. No government erected by man has that right.

We're tired of waiting; every time black people try to move in this country, they're forced to defend their position beforehand. It's time for white people to start defending themselves as to why they have oppressed and exploited us.

I am black, therefore I am. Not I am black and I must go to college to prove myself. I am black, therefore I am. And don't deprive me of anything and say to me that you must go to college before you gain access to X, Y, and Z. That's only a rationalization for oppression.

It is sometimes ironic that many of the peace groups have begun to call SNCC violent and they say they can no longer support us, when we are in fact the most militant organization for peace or civil rights or human rights against the war in Vietnam in this country today.

We must begin, as the philosopher Camus says, to come alive by saying "no." This country is a nation of thieves. It stole everything it has, beginning with black people. The U.S. cannot justify its existence as the policeman of the world any longer.

We have found all the myths of the country to be nothing but downright lies. We were told that if we worked hard we would succeed, and if that were true we would own this country lock, stock, and barrel. We have picked the cotton for nothing; we are the maids in the kitchens of liberal white people; we are the janitors, the porters, the elevator men; we sweep up your college floors.

We must question the values of this society, and I maintain that black people are the best people to do that since we have been excluded from that society. We ought to think whether or not we want to become a part of that society. And because black people are saying we do not now want to become a part of you, we are called reverse racists. Ain't that a gas?

White society has caused the failure of nonviolence. I was always surprised at Quakers who came to Alabama and counseled me to be nonviolent, but didn't have the guts to tell the Sheriff in Selma, Alabama to be nonviolent. Can you name one black man today who has killed anybody white and is still alive? Even after a rebellion, when some black brothers throw bricks and bottles, ten thousand of them have to pay the price. When the white policeman comes in, anybody who's black is arrested because we all look alike.

As Thomas Jefferson said, "The God who gave us life, gave us liberty at the same time; no King holds the right of liberty in his hands." Nor does any ruler in American government. This nation was never meant to be a unit of one, but a united of the many. That is the exact reason our freedom loving forefathers established the states, so as to divide the rights and powers among the states, insuring that no central power could gain master government control.

And so it was meant in our racial lives. Each race, within its own framework, has the freedom to teach, to instruct, to develop, to ask for and receive deserved help from others of separate racial stations. This is the great freedom of our American founding fathers. But if we amalgamate into the one unit as advocated by the communist philosophers, then the enrichment of our lives—the freedom for our development— is gone forever. We become, therefore, a mongrel unit of one under a single all powerful government. We stand for everything and for nothing.

The true brotherhood of America, of respecting the separateness of others and uniting in effort, has been so twisted and distorted from its original concept that there is a small wonder that communism is winning the world.

This country assumes that if someone is poor, they are poor because of their own individual blight, or they weren't born on the right side of town, or they had too many children, or went in the army too early, or because their father was a drunk, or they didn't care about school—*they* made a mistake. That's a lot of nonsense. Poverty is well calculated in this country, and the reason why the poverty program won't work is because the calculators of poverty are administering it.

We have developed a movement in the black community. The white activist has miserably failed to develop the movement inside of his community. Will white people have the courage to go into the white communities and start organizing them? That's the question for the white activist. We won't get caught up in questions about power. This country knows what power is. It knows what Black Power is because it deprived black people of it for over four hundred years. White people associate Black Power with violence because of their own inability to deal with blackness. If we had said "Negro power" nobody would get scared. Everybody would support it.

> **We invite the negro citizens of Alabama to work with us from his separate racial station and we will work with him to develop, to grow in individual freedom and enrichment.**
>
> **But we warn those, of any group, who would follow the false doctrine of communistic amalgamation that we will not surrender our system of government. Our freedom of race and religion was won at a hard price and if it requires a hard price to retain it then we are able, and quite willing, to pay it.**
>
> **The liberals' theory that poverty, discrimination and lack of opportunity is the cause of communism is a false theory. If it were true the South would have been the biggest single communist bloc in the western hemisphere long ago; for after the great War between the States, our people faced a desolate land of burned universities, destroyed crops and homes, with manpower depleted and crippled. There were no government handouts, no Marshall Plan aid, no coddling to make sure that our people would not suffer; instead the South was set upon by the vulturous carpetbagger and federal troops, all loyal Southerners were denied the vote at the point of bayonet, so that the infamous, illegal 14th Amendment might be passed. There was no money, no food and no hope of either. But our grandfathers bent their knee only in church and bowed their head only to God.**

Not for a single instant did they ever consider the easy way of federal dictatorship and amalgamation in return for fat bellies. They fought. They dug sweet roots from the ground with their bare hands and boiled them in iron pots. They gathered poke salad from the woods and acorns from the ground. They fought. They followed no false doctrine—they knew what they wanted and they fought for freedom! They came up from their knees in the greatest display of sheer nerve, grit and guts that has ever been set down in the pages of written history ... and they won! The great writer, Rudyard Kipling wrote of them, that: "There in the Southland of the United States of America, lives the greatest fighting breed of man in all the world!

I look at Dr. King on television every single day, and I say to myself: "Now there is a man who's desperately needed in this country. There is a man full of love. There is a man full of mercy. There is a man full of compassion." But every time I see Lyndon on television, I say, "Martin, baby, you got a long way to go."

If we were to be real and honest, we would have to admit that most people in this country see things black and white. White people would have to admit that they are afraid to go into a black ghetto at night. They're afraid because they'd be "beat up," "lynched," "looted," "cut up," etc. It happens to black people inside the ghetto every day, incidentally. Since white people are afraid of that, they get a man to do it for them—a policeman. Figure his mentality. The first time a black man jumps, that white man's going to shoot him. Police brutality is going to exist on that level. The only time I hear people talk about nonviolence is when black people move to defend themselves against white people. White people beat up black people every day— nobody talks about nonviolence.

... The question is how we're going to organize our way, whether it's going to be done with a thousand policemen with submachine guns, or whether it's going to be done in a context where it's allowed by white people warding off those policemen. Are white people who call themselves activists ready to move into the white communities to build new political institutions to destroy the old ones? If so, then we can start to build a new world. This country is a nation of thieves. It stands on the brink of becoming a nation of murderers. We must stop it. We must stop it.

We are on the move for our liberation. We're tired of trying to prove things to white people. We are tired of trying to explain to white people that we're not going to hurt them. We are concerned with getting the things we want, the things we have to have to be able to function. Will white people overcome their racism and allow for that to happen in this country? If not, we have no choice but to say very clearly,

And that is why today, I stand ashamed of the fat, well-fed whimperers who say that it is inevitable, that our cause is lost. I am ashamed of them and I am ashamed for them. They do not represent the people of the Southland. Southerners played a most magnificent part in erecting this great divinely inspired system of freedom and as God is our witnesses, Southerners will save it.

I will apply the old sound rule of our fathers, that anything worthy of our defense is worthy of one hundred percent of our defense. I have been taught that freedom meant freedom from any threat or fear of government. I was born in that freedom, I was raised in that freedom . . . I intend to live in that freedom . . . and God willing, when I die, I shall leave that freedom to my children . . . as my father left it to me.

So help me God.

And my prayer is that the Father who "Move on over,
reigns above us will bless all the people or we're going to
of this great sovereign State and nation, move over you."
both white and black.

I thank you.

Alabama Governor George Wallace attempts to physically prevent racial integration at the University of Alabama, June 11, 1963.

Luke and Bo Duke evade police in General Lee, their car, in the television show *Dukes of Hazzard*, which ran 1979–1985.

Radio Raheem tells the story of life in Spike Lee's *Do the Right Thing*, 1989.

Don't you dare go runnin' down my little town where I grew up
And I won't cuss your city lights
If you ain't ever took a ride around
And cruised right through the heart of my town
Anything you say would be a lie
We may live our lives a little slower
But that don't mean I wouldn't be proud to show ya'

Where I come from
The pine trees are singing a song of the south
Where I come from
That little white church is gonna have a crowd
Yeah, I'm pretty damn proud of where I come from.

Where I come from
There's a big ole moon shining down at night
Where I come from
There's a man done wrong gonna make it right
Where I come from
There's an old farm boy out turning up dirt
Where I come from

The end of the world only means the end of a certain "power." The end of colonialism ends the world of the colonizer.

Justice only means that the wicked slave master must reap the fruit (or harvest) of the evil seeds of slavery he has planted. This is justice! Other slave empires received justice, and now White America must receive justice. According to White America's own evil past, which is clearly recorded on the pages of history, so shall God judge her today.

The white liberal differs from the white conservative only in one way: the liberal is more deceitful than the conservative. The liberal is more hypocritical than the conservative. Both want power, but the white liberal is the one who has perfected the art of posing as the Negro's friend and benefactor; and by winning the friendship, allegiance, and support of the Negro, the white liberal is able to use the Negro as a pawn or tool in this political "football game" that is constantly raging between the white liberals and white conservatives.

Politically the American Negro is nothing but a football and the white liberals control this mentally dead ball through tricks of tokenism: false promises of integration and civil rights. In this profitable game of deceiving and exploiting the political politician of the American Negro, those white liberals have the willing cooperation of the Negro civil rights leaders. These "leaders" sell out our people for just a few crumbs of token recognition and token gains. These "leaders" are satisfied with token victories and token progress because they themselves are nothing but token leaders.

The white conservatives are like wolves; they show their teeth in a snarl that keeps the Negro always aware of where he stands with them. But the white liberals are foxes, who also show their teeth to the Negro but pretend that they are smiling. The white liberals are more dangerous than the conservatives; they lure the Negro, and as the Negro runs from the growling wolf, he flees into the open jaws of the "smiling" fox.

The white liberals control the Negro by controlling the Negro civil rights leaders and thus control and contain the Negro's struggle, and they can control the Negro's so-called revolt. The Negro "revolution" is controlled by these foxy white liberals, by the government itself.

The *black* revolution is the struggle of the nonwhites of this earth against their white oppressors. Revolutions are based upon land. Revolutionaries are the landless against the landlord. Revolutions are never peaceful, never loving, never nonviolent. Nor are they ever compromising. Revolutions are destructive and bloody. Revolutionaries don't compromise with the enemy; they don't even negotiate. Like the flood in Noah's day, revolution drowns all opposition, or like the fire in Lot's day, the black revolution burns everything that gets in its path.

America is the stronghold of white supremacy. The black revolution is sweeping down upon America like a raging forest fire. It is only a matter of time before America herself will be engulfed by the black flames.

The black masses across the country at the grassroots level have already begun to take their cases to the streets on their own. The government in Washington knew that something had to be done to get the rampaging Negroes back into the corral, back under the control of the white liberals.

The government propaganda machine began encouraging Negroes to follow only what it calls "responsible" Negro leaders. The government actually means Negro leaders who are responsible to the government, and who can therefore be controlled by the government, and be used by that same government to control their impatient people.

Example: If I have a cup of coffee that is too strong for me because it is too black, I weaken it by pouring cream into it, I integrate it with cream. If I keep pouring enough cream in the coffee, pretty soon the entire flavor of the coffee is changed; the very nature of the coffee is changed. If enough cream is poured in, eventually you don't even know that I had coffee in this cup. This is what happened with the March on Washington. The whites didn't integrate it; they infiltrated it. Whites joined it; they engulfed it; they became so much a part of it, it lost its original flavor. It ceased to be a black march; it ceased to be militant; it ceased to be angry; it ceased to be impatient. In fact, it ceased to be a march. It became a picnic, an outing with a festive, circus-like atmosphere… CLOWNS AND ALL.

Supporters of Darren Wilson, police officer who killed Michael Brown, August 23, 2015.

&rlz=1C5CHFA_enUS508US508&espv=2&biw=133...

heath

SafeSearch

Billboard for US Black Chambers and University of Phoenix's luncheon "From Black Panthers to Black Lives Matter," featuring Deray McKesson, sponsored by Wells Fargo, 2016.

Madame Binh Graphics Collective / Republic of New Afrika, *Assata Shakur is Welcome Here*, 1979-80. The poster was displayed in windows in Harlem, Brownsville, Bed-Stuy, and South Bronx after Shakur escaped from prison in 1979.

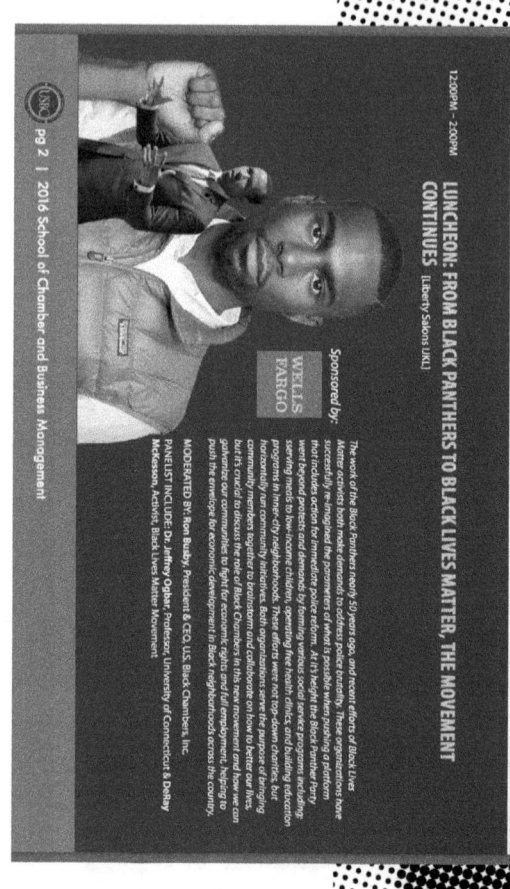

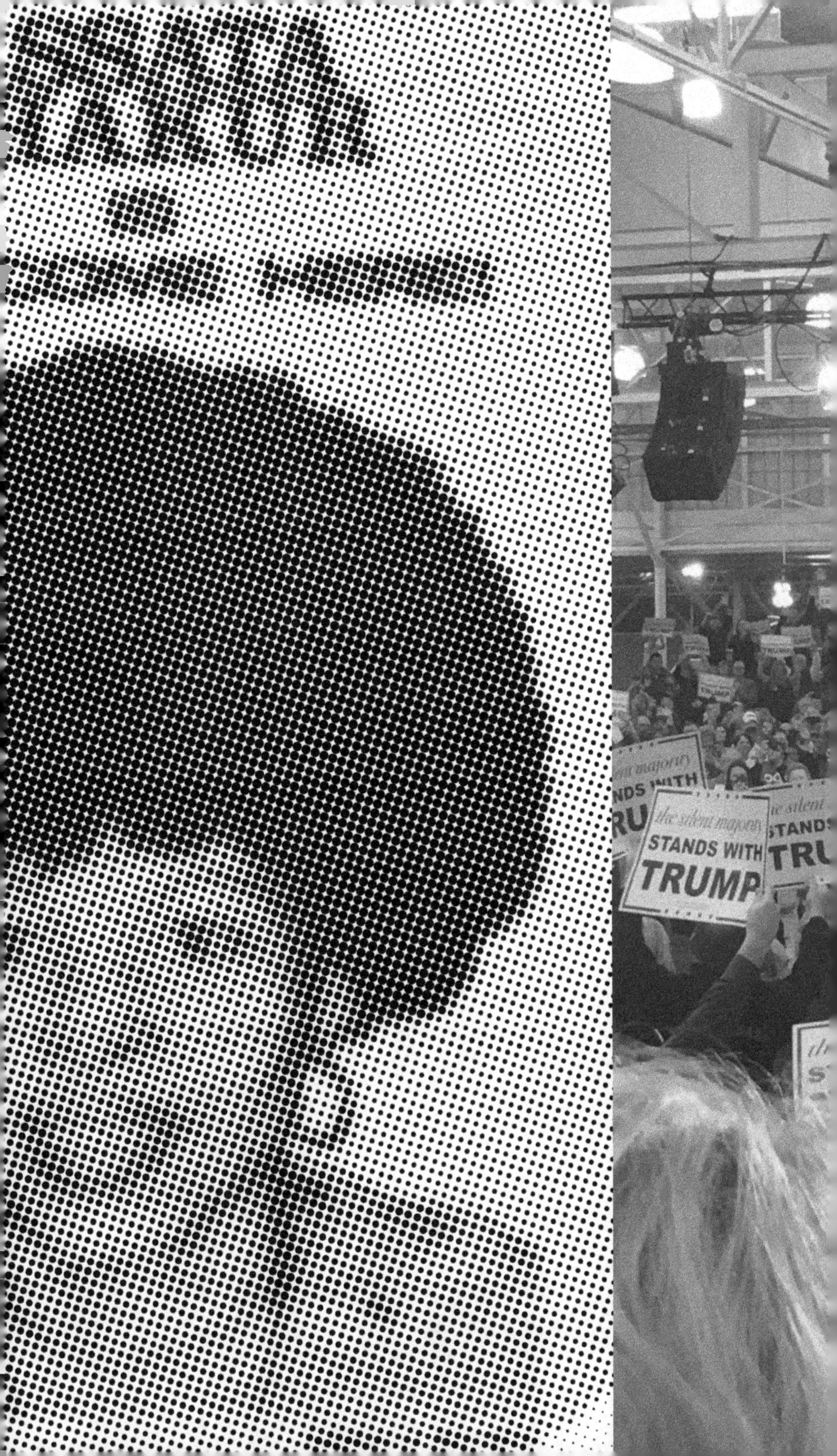
the silent majority
STANDS WITH
TRUMP

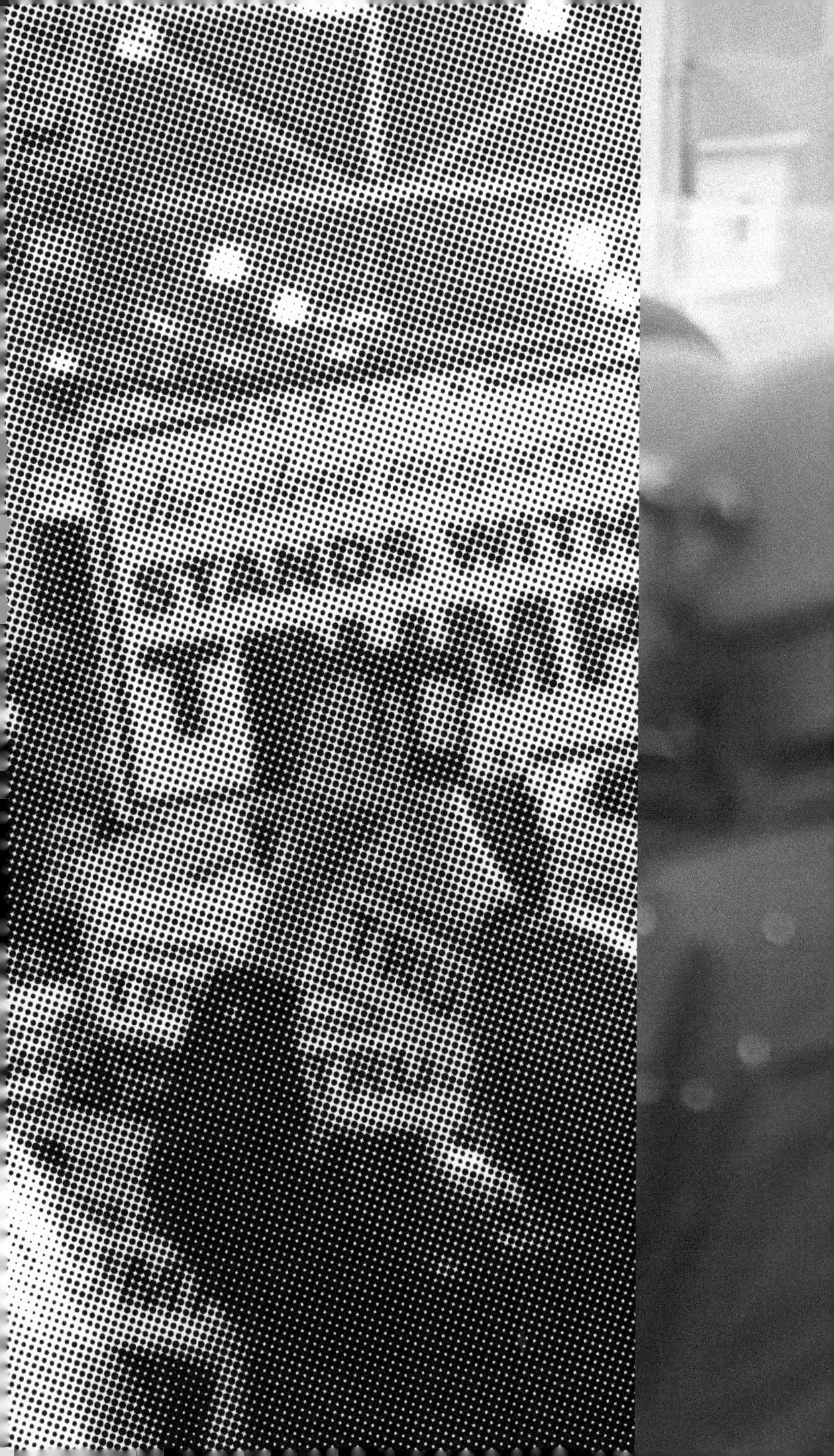

Let me tell you the story of right hand / left hand. It is a story of Good and Evil. HATE—the left hand—it was with this hand that Cain iced his brother. LOVE—the right hand, these five fingers—they go straight to the soul of man. The right hand of *love*. One hand is always fightin' the other hand; this is the story of life. Static. Your left hand is kickin' much ass and it looks like your right hand, *love*, is finished. But hold on, stop the presses. The right hand is comin' back. Yea, he got the left hand on the ropes. Ooooh! that's a devastatin' right and HATE is *down*. Ooooh! Damn! Left hand is KO'd by LOVE.

If I love you, I *love* you. But if I hate you...

this was an assault on the american way of life, the american justice system... the american police officer is strong, we will continue to fight, we will continue to sacrifice ourselves for good law abiding people for every community in the united states.

Hello. This is Bernardine Dohrn.

I'm going to read a
DECLARATION OF A STATE OF WAR

All over the world, people fighting Amerikan imperialism look to Amerika's youth to use our strategic position behind enemy lines to join forces in the destruction of the empire.

Black people have been fighting almost alone for years. We've known that our job is to lead white kids into armed revolution. Kids know the *lines are drawn*, revolution is touching all of our lives. Tens of thousands have learned that protest and marches don't do it.

Ché taught us that "revolutionaries move like fish in the sea." The alienation and contempt that young people have for this country has created the ocean for this revolution.

The parents of "privileged" kids have been saying for years that the revolution was a game for us. But the war and the racism of this society show that it is too fucked-up. We will never live peaceably under this system.

The twelve Weathermen who were indicted for leading last October's riots in Chicago have never left the country. Terry is dead, Linda was captured by a pig informer, but the rest of us move freely in and out of every city and youth scene in this country. We're not hiding out but we're invisible.

If you want to find us, this is where we are. In every tribe, commune, dormitory, farmhouse, barracks and townhouse where kids are making love, smoking dope and loading guns— fugitives from Amerikan justice are free to go.

Never again will they fight alone.

Minneapolis Police Chief Janeé Harteau holds a rock ostensibly thrown at police during protests following the killing of Jamar Clark by police officers, November 19, 2015.

Black men on the south side of Chicago prepare for guerilla warfare in Sam Greenlee and Ivan Dixon's fantasy film *The Spook Who Sat by the Door*, 1973.

This is the underlying surplus on which riots rest: a racialized surplus population, unable to be absorbed into the circuits of production. The management of this population looks like ghettoization, hyperincarceration, increasingly brutal policing—"the state-sanctioned or extralegal production and exploitation of group-differentiated vulnerability to premature death," in Ruth Wilson Gilmore's practical definition of racism. The circulation struggle and the race riot are one. "Race is the modality in which class is lived."

As president of the United States, I would be untrue to my oath of office if I allowed the policy of this nation to be dictated by the minority who hold that point of view and would try to impose it on the nation by mounting demonstrations in the street. So tonight, to you, the great silent majority of my fellow Americans I ask for your support.

It is time for the silent majority in this country to support law enforcement. There are a few bad apples in every profession. That does not mean that there should be open warfare declared on law enforcement. The vast majority of officers are there to do the right thing; are there because they care about their community and want to make it a safer place. What happened last night is an assault on the very fabric of society. It is time to come forward and support law enforcement and condemn this atrocious act.

The economy was once near, with most subsistence goods produced nearby. Conversely the state was far, so to speak; modern policing did not exist. Now the situation is reversed. Everything is produced elsewhere; there's a cop around every corner. The idea that one could make one's way via the sacking of the shopping district is absurd on the face of it; you might get subsistence goods for a week, two, a month, and then what? The cereal bearer in this way captures both sides of the matter: the truth of the riot, and its limit.

32

I am too pissed off tonight to be diplomatic about what is going on and I'm not going to stick my head in the sand about it. I said last December that war had been declared on the American police officer. It is open season right now there is no doubt about it. Any time a police officer is killed a little of every police officer dies along with them. I need every law abiding person to stand up and start pushing back	against this slime, this filth that is disparaging the American law enforcement. Demand people that belong to these organizations to get out of town—there's no room for it. The American police officer is holding these communities together and we need the support from people that we defend every day in order to get that done. God bless the Harris County Sheriff's office—kudos to that district attorney for acknowledging the war on police. **But as with all such dialectical reversals, there is another reversal in store. The limit of the riot bears the riot's potentialities within it. Survival, reproduction of the immiserated classes can no longer be obtained in the market— can no longer even be imagined there. And it is because of this desperate situation that we can imagine circulation struggles breaking their attachment to the market, turning toward struggles over reproduction beyond wage and price. It is here we encounter the figure of the commune, the tactic which is also a form of life: social reproduction beyond wage and market both. That is the dream that the riot dreams.**

Grandma's hands clapped in church on Sunday morning
Grandma's hands played the tambourine so well
Grandma's hands used to issue out a warning
She'd say, "Billy don't you run so fast
Might fall on a piece of glass
Might be snakes there in that grass"
Grandma's hands

Grandma's hands soothed the local unwed mother
Grandma's hands used to ache sometimes and swell
Grandma's hands used to lift her face and tell her
She'd say, "Baby, Grandma understands
That you really loved that man
Put yourself in Jesus' hands"
Grandma's Hands

Grandma's hands used to hand me piece of candy
Grandma's hands picked me up each time I fell
Grandma's hands, boy they really came in handy
She'd say, "Mattie don't you whip that boy
What you want to spank him for?
He didn't drop no apple core"
But I don't have Grandma anymore

If I get to heaven I'll look for
Grandma's hands

Still from Peter Watkins' film *La Commune (Paris 1871)*, 2000.

We bring the Commune with us to the barricades.

Police enter Oaxaca after attacking striking teachers' encampment blockading the Oaxaca State Institute of Public Education, June 11, 2016.

Police protect CVS from "looters," April 27, 2015.

we've heard
'black lives matter,' and
'all lives matter'—
well, cops' lives matter, too.

so why don't we just
drop the qualifier and say
'lives matter,' and take
that to the bank.

Here's how I would handle the race thing? You start out—and now y'all aren't quoting me on this, are you?

You start out in 1954 by saying, 'n*gger, n*gger, n*gger.' By 1968, you can't say 'n*gger'; that hurts you. It backfires. So you say stuff like 'forced busing,' 'states' rights,' and all that stuff. And you're getting so abstract now, you're talking about cutting taxes, and all of these things you're talking about are totally economic things, and a byproduct of them is, blacks get hurt worse than whites. And subconsciously, maybe that is part of it; I'm not saying that. But I'm saying that if it is getting that abstract and that coded that we're doing away with the racial problem one way or the other. You follow me? Because obviously sitting around saying 'we want to cut taxes,' 'we want to cut this,' and 'we want that' is much more abstract than even the busing thing, and a hell of a lot more abstract than 'n*gger, n*gger.' You know.

So any way you look at it, race is coming on the back burner.

A lot of people called it prison when I was growin' up
But these are my roots and this is what I love
'Cause everybody knows me and I know them
And I believe that's the way we were supposed to live
Wouldn't trade one single day here in small town, USA

Give me a Saturday night my baby by my side
A little Hank Jr. and a six pack of Light
Old dirt road and I'll be just fine

Give me a Sunday morning that's full of grace
A simple life and I'll be okay
Here in small town, USA

Around here we break our backs just to earn a buck
We never get ahead but we have enough
I watch people leave and then come right back
I never wanted any part of that
I'm proud to say that I love this place
Good ole small town, USA

Give me a Saturday night my baby by my side
David Allen Coe and a six pack of Light
Old dirt road and I'll be just fine

Give me a Sunday morning that's full of grace
A simple life and I'll be okay
Here in small town, USA
Oh yeah

I wouldn't trade one single day
I'm proud to say I love this place

Give me a Saturday night my baby by my side
"Sweet Home Alabama" and a six pack of Light
Old dirt road and I'll be just fine
Give me a Sunday morning that's full of grace

A simple life and I'll be okay
Yeah I'll be okay
Here in small town, USA
Oh yeah small town, USA

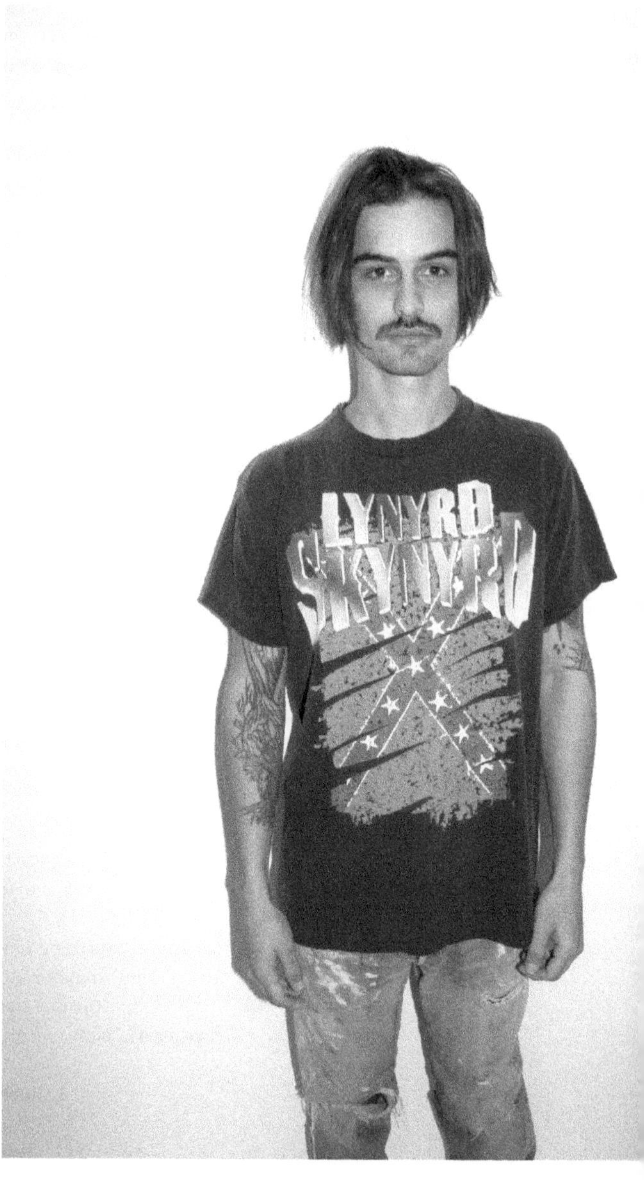
LYNYRD
SKYNYRD

43

Dear Ta-Nehisi Coates,

When you talk about revolution, most people think about violence without realizing that the real content of any kind of revolutionary thrust lies in the principles and the goals that you are striving for. Not in the way you reach them. On the other hand, because of the way this society is organized, because of the violence that exists on the surface everywhere, you have to expect that there are going to be such explosions.

When I was living in Los Angeles, long before I became known to the police as a revolutionary, I was constantly stopped and harassed by the police. They didn't know who I was but I was a black woman with a natural and I suppose they thought I might be a "militant." When you live under a situation like that constantly, and then you ask me whether I approve of violence... that just doesn't make any sense at all. Whether I approve of guns!

I grew up in Birmingham, Alabama and some very good friends of mine were killed by bombs—bombs that were planted by racists. I remember, from the time I was very small, the sounds of bombs exploding across the street. I remember our house shaking. I remember my father having to have guns at his disposal at all times because of the fact that at any moment we might expect to be attacked. The man who was in control at that time—Bull Connor—would often get on the radio and make statements like: "n*ggers have moved into a white neighborhood; we better expect some bloodshed tonight." And sure enough there would be bloodshed. In a well known incident, four young black girls were killed in a bomb explosion in Birmingham. One lived next door to me; my family was close to all of them. In fact when the bombing occurred, one girl's mother called my mother to ask: "Can you take me down to the church to pick up Carol? We heard about the bombing and I don't have my car." And what they found when they got there was limbs and heads strewn all over the place.

The disturbing challenge of your book is your rejection of the American Dream. You write to your son, "Here is what I would like for you to know: In America, it is traditional to destroy the black body—it is heritage." The innocent world of the dream is actually built on the broken bodies of those kept down below.

If there were no black bodies to oppress, the affluent Dreamers "would have to determine how to build their suburbs on something other than human bones, how to angle their jails toward something other than a human stockyard, how to erect a democracy independent of cannibalism."

Your definition of "white" is complicated. But you write "'White America' is a syndicate arrayed to protect its exclusive power to dominate and control our bodies. Sometimes this power is direct (lynching), and sometimes it is insidious (redlining)." In what is bound to be the most quoted passage from the book, you write that you watched the smoldering towers of 9/11 with a cold heart. At the time you felt the police and firefighters who died "were menaces of nature; they were the fire, the comet, the storm, which could—with no justification—shatter my body."

You obviously do not mean that literally today (sometimes in your phrasing you seem determined to be misunderstood).

44

After that all of the men in my neighborhood organized themselves into an armed patrol. They had to take their guns and patrol our community every night because they did not want that to happen in our community again. That is why when someone asks me about violence... I just find it incredible, because what it means is that the person who is asking has absolutely no idea what black people have gone through, what black people have experienced in this country since the time the first black person was kidnapped from the shores of Africa.

You are illustrating the perspective born of the rage "that burned in me then, animates me now, and will likely leave me on fire for the rest of my days."

I have to ask, am I displaying my privilege if I disagree? Does a white person have standing to respond?

I think you distort American history. This country, like each person in it, is a mixture of glory and shame. There's a Lincoln for every Jefferson Davis. Violence is embedded in America, but it is not close to the totality of America.

In your anger you reject the American dream itself as flimflam. But a dream sullied is not a lie. The American dream of equal opportunity, social mobility and ever more perfect democracy cherishes the future more than the past. It abandons old wrongs and transcends old sins for the sake of a better tomorrow.

This dream is a secular faith that has unified people across every known divide. It has unleashed ennobling energies and mobilized heroic social reform movements. By dissolving the dream under the acid of an excessive realism, you trap generations in the past and destroy the guiding star that points to a better future.

Maybe you will find my reactions irksome. Maybe the right white response is just silence for a change.

'Muslim-free' gun store se... × | George Zimmerman: Trayv... × | Fla. wo

← → C | www.cbsnews.com/news/fla-woman-marissa-alexander-gets-20

HOW CAN TAX-EFFIC
INVESTING GROW Y
ASSETS IN 20 YEAR

By JULIA DAHL / CBS NEWS / May 16, 2012, 4:21 PM

Fla. woman Marissa A gets 20 years for "war Did she stand her grou

Marissa Alexander / **KYTX**

3 Comments / 966 Shares / Tweet / Stumble /

2035 Click to find out ▶

nder
shot":

Follow Us
f / 🐦 /

I'M WITH ➤ER

Add my name

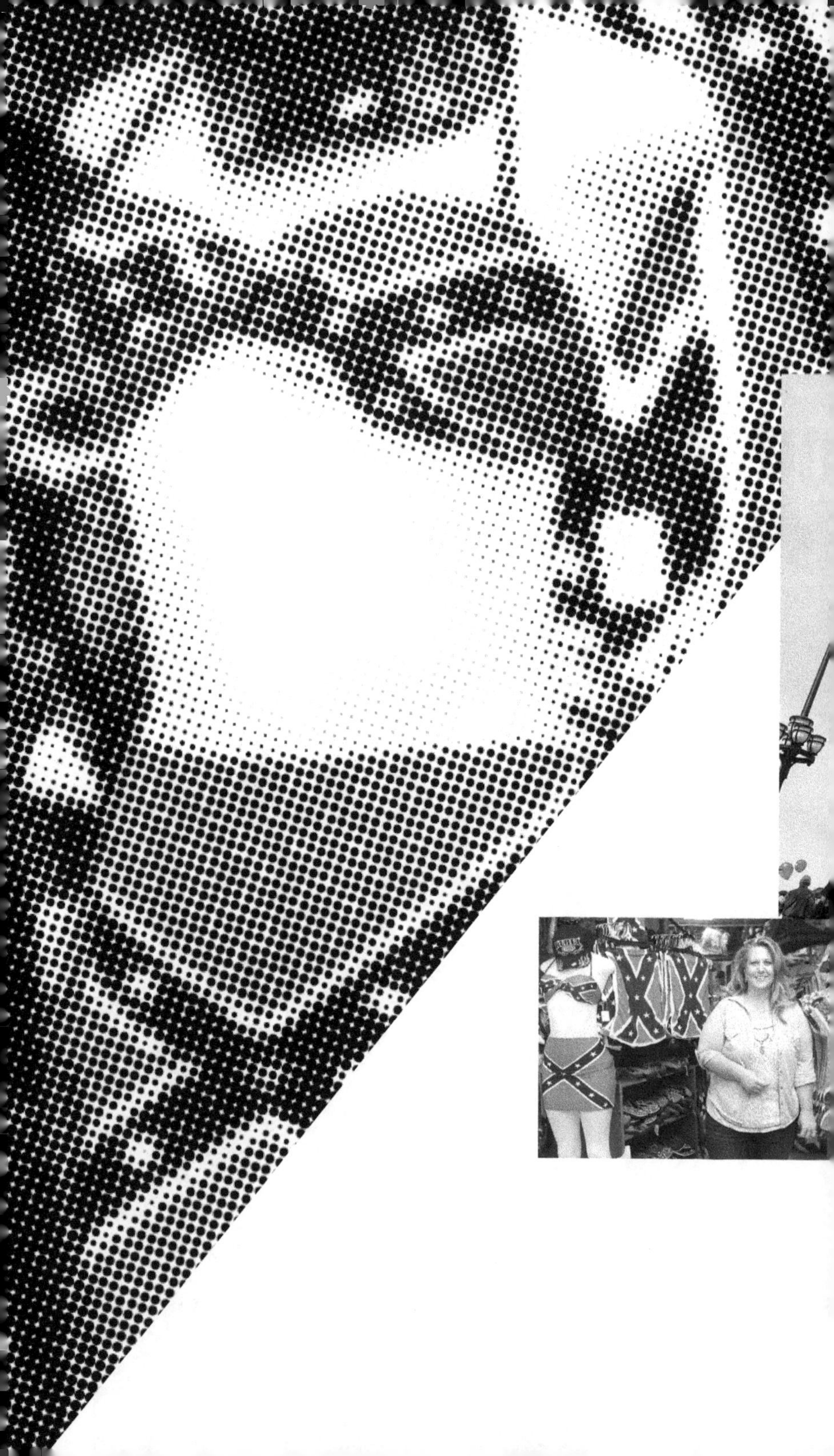

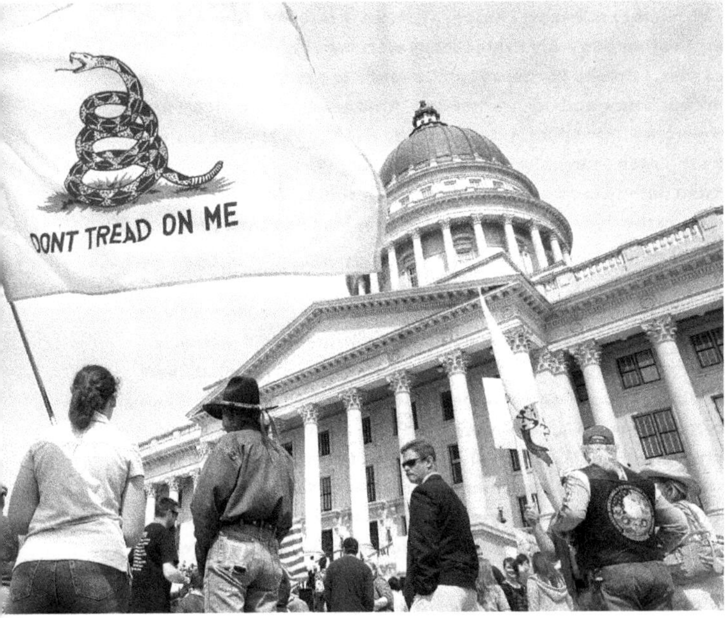
DONT TREAD ON ME

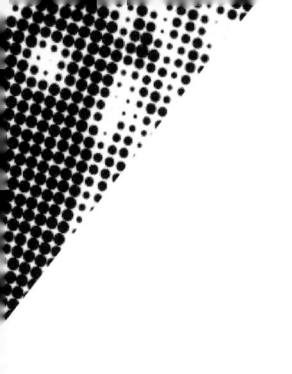

Like many of you here I grew up in a small town.

My dad was a preacher at a local church; my mom was a part-time secretary and raised my brother and I. My first job was working at the Countryside Restaurant. Later, I flipped burgers at McDonald's to pay my way through college. I look back now and my brother and I kind of laugh. We didn't know it then but we were kind of poor. I think looking ahead as Republicans we need to make the case that we're going to promote policies that promote and support and defend hard work in this country again. We need to promote policies that open the door of opportunity for people to live their piece of the American dream.

Growing up in Wisconsin I never heard one of my classmates say: "Hey Scott, when I grow up, I want to be dependent on the government." America is one of the few places left in the world where it doesn't matter what class you were born into. The ultimate outcome is up to each and every individual. You see, there is a reason why in America we take a day off to celebrate the Fourth of July and not the Fifteenth of April, because in America we value our independence from the government not our dependence on it! To keep that going forward we need leaders in Washington who understand it is important to build the economy in cities and towns all across this great country. We need a president who understands that when freedom loving people anywhere in the world are under attack anywhere we are all under attack. We need leaders who will stand with our allies against radical Islamic terrorists! We need leaders in America who understand the measure of success in government is not how many people are dependent on the government, the measure of success in government is how many people are no longer dependent on the government.

Farmers pull down police barricade in Brussels outside EU headquarters, September 7, 2015.

Dear T.C.,

I was just thinking about the night they said you did the crime. You remember it was the same night that you had the real bad nightmare. Why didn't they believe you was here with me? Ol' riff-raff me. You don't even look like the man they said did it—but you're still doin' the time. So much has happened T.C.. T.C. ... they beat our baby out of me. They wouldn't let me see nobody, not even a doctor, for ten days. We got to make changes T.C. so we can raise our kids with both of us at home so things go right. I've been blaming myself all this time 'cause things wasn't right. I thought that I was born to be poor, to be pushed around and stepped on. I don't want Lou Anne thinkin' like that. I can see now that my problem is the place I was born into—a place with laws that protect the people who got money. Doctors in hospitals for people who got money.

On behalf of the Support Darren Wilson Campaign, we want to thank those in attendance as well as vocal supporters from around the world, for publicly displaying your support for Darren Wilson. Our mission is to formally declare that we share the united belief that Officer Wilson's actions on August 9, 2014, were warranted and justified. He has our unwavering support.

We believe the evidence has and will continue to validate our position. We want to thank the media for finally highlighting the other side of this story. However, the media has shown a strong bias against the supporters of Darren Wilson. We believe this has only intensified the destruction of the community of Ferguson and the surrounding St. Louis areas. We are exclusively here to support Darren Wilson, and have no desire to engage in the negativity and hate which has paralyzed Officer Wilson's duty to pursue justice. Many of us have received death threats against ourselves and our families.

It's evil and wrong. I have to get to know myself, to read and to study. We all have to so we can change it, so we can know how to talk to each other. Talking to each other is not easy. I know you in jail, T.C., and angry, but most of the time I don't understand your letters. Talk to me easy T.C. 'cause I want to understand. It's not easy to win over people like me. There's a lot of people like me—we have many things to fight for just to live. But the idea is to win over more of our people. Talk the same talk but easy. T.C. ... You remember you used to ask why I always wear a wig? All day and all night, when I eat, when I sleep. T.C. ... the wig is off my head. The wig is off my head. I never saw what was under it, I just saw on top the wig. The wig is off my head T.C. ...

T.C., I love you.

Dorothy

Contrary to media suggestions, we are not affiliated with any hate groups. However we respect each individual's first amendment rights in this country.

We will not hide. We will no longer live in fear. We ask this question: "Can justice ever be attained if one side's supporters are living in fear of speaking out?" If you support Darren Wilson make your voices heard. Call or write Governor Jay Nixon and demand that this bias stops now! [cheers]

At the end of this statement the media will inevitably ask for my name and others' names and relationships, job titles, stories, etc. You want my name: my name is Darren Wilson! We are Darren Wilson!

53

55

the biggest pain in the ass, is that you're still here recording, watching everything but not giving a fuck. whether it's a film or reality, you just stand there and i'd like to kill that!

you think i don't give a fuck?

often you don't, otherwise you'd be with us. you hide behind your tv and watch us die off. you have to join us! drop your microphone. fight with us for utopias. there are still some left to defend.

i hate war. but i hate our enemies even more. they despise us, have no mercy, so neither do we. today we are our own barricade and not to fight means dying inside. we bring the commune with us to the barricades. it's our choice and our freedom. thanks to the struggle.

that's all i wanted to say.

Credits

P. 0. Reformulation of Guy Debord, *The Society of the Spectacle*, Thesis 203
BOPSECRETS.ORG/SI/DEBORD/

P. 1. Guy Debord, *The Society of the Spectacle*, Thesis 131
BOPSECRETS.ORG/SI/DEBORD/

P. 2–3. Walter Benjamin, "Theses on the Philosophy of History," Thesis V
MARXISTS.ORG/REFERENCE/ARCHIVE/BENJAMIN/1940/HISTORY.HTM

P. 4–5. *image:* Confederate flags at University of Mississippi football game

P. 4. Brief excerpt from Ta-Nehisi Coates "The Return of the Black Panther: A Behind the Scenes Look at the Revival of Marvel's first black-superhero series"
THEATLANTIC.COM/MAGAZINE/ARCHIVE/2016/04/THE-RETURN-OF-THE-BLACK-PANTHER/471516/

P. 4. 1966 ABC news report on the "Aftermath of Watts"
YOUTUBE.COM/WATCH?V=7JQHFZV-CMS

P. 6–15. Stokely Carmichael speaks at University of California, Berkeley, 1966
BLACKPAST.ORG/1966-STOKELY-CARMICHAEL-BLACK-POWER-0

P. 6–15. Alabama Governor George Wallace's Inaugural Address, 1963
WEB.UTK.EDU/~MFITZGE1/DOCS/374/WALLACE_SEG63.PDF

P. 6–7. *image:* Watts uprising, aerial view, 1965

P. 7. *image:* Watts uprising, police patrol at night, 1965

P. 16–17. *image:* Alabama Governor George Wallace attempts to physically prevent racial integration at the University of Alabama, June 11, 1963
YOUTUBE.COM/WATCH?V=L1RD6XFGG5S

P. 17. *image:* Still of "General Lee," the famous confederate flag car from the television show *Dukes of Hazard*, which ran 1979-1985

P. 18–19. *image:* Still of Radio Raheem from Spike Lee's *Do the Right Thing*, 1989

P. 19. Montgomery Gentry, "Where I Come From" lyrics, 2011
YOUTUBE.COM/WATCH?V=BR98A-D4690G&LIST=RDBR98AD4690G

P. 20–21. Malcolm X, "God's Judgement of White America (The Chickens Come Home to Roost)," 1964
MALCOLM-X.ORG/SPEECHES/SPC_120463.HTM

P. 22–23. *image:* Google Image search of "sharpton ferguson"

P. 22. *image:* Darren Wilson supporters rally in Ferguson, Missouri, August 2015
YOUTUBE.COM/WATCH?V=4UCVN4IZNQC

P. 24. *image:* Billboard for US Black Chambers and University of Phoenix's luncheon "From Black Panthers to Black Lives Matter," featuring Deray McKesson sponsored by Wells Fargo, 2016

P. 24–25. *image:* "Assata is Welcome Here" poster by Madame Binh Graphics Collective / Republic of New Afrika, 1979–80

P. 25–26. *image:* "The Silent Majority Stands with Trump," Donald Trump Campaign rally, 2015

P. 26–27. *image:* Behind police lines in Baltimore, 2015

p. 27. Transcript from "The Story of Love and Hate" as told by Radio Raheem in Spike Lee's *Do the Right Thing*, 1989
YOUTUBE.COM/WATCH?V=PA-OUPTR9LI
I'm indebted to Anarchist Without Content and *Hostis: A Journal of Incivility* to bringing Radio Raheem to my attention.
ANARCHISTWITHOUTCONTENT.WORDPRESS.COM/2015/08/28/IN-DEFENSE-OF-CRUELTY/

p. 28. Milwaukee County Sheriff David Clarke on Fox News, August 29, 2015
YOUTUBE.COM/WATCH?V=Q1Z9XYGZTFC

p. 29. Communique #1 from the Weather Underground, 1970
SDS-1960S.ORG/SDS_WUO/WEATHER/WUO_COMMUNIQUE_1.TXT

p. 30–31. *image:* Minneapolis Police Chief Janee Harteau holds a rock, ostensibly thrown at police during protests, at press conference following the killing of Jamar Clark by police officers, November 19, 2015

p. 30–31. *image:* Still from Sam Greenlee and Ivan Dixon's film *The Spook Who Sat by the Door*, 1973.

p. 32–33. Joshua Clover, "Baltimore Riot. Baltimore Commune?" 2016
VERSOBOOKS.COM/BLOGS/2614-BALTIMORE-RIOT-BALTIMORE-COMMUNE

p. 32–33. Various excerpts regarding "the silent majority" including: Richard Nixon, November 3, 1969; Harris County Sheriff Ron Hickman, August 29, 2015; Milwaukee County Sheriff David Clarke, August 29, 2015
Nixon: YOUTUBE.COM/WATCH?V=HQZ0183JQXG
Hickman: YOUTUBE.COM/WATCH?V=ZFICPJ5CUA0
Clarke: YOUTUBE.COM/WATCH?V=Q1Z9X-YGZTFC

p. 34. Bill Withers, "Grandma's Hands" lyrics, 1971

p. 35. *image:* Still from Peter Watkins' film *La Commune (Paris 1871)*, 2000

p. 36–37. *image:* Police enter Oaxaca after attacking striking teachers' encampment blockading the Oaxaca State Institute of Public Education, June 11, 2016
ITSGOINGDOWN.ORG/POLICE-ATTACK-BARRICADES-REAPPEAR-OAXACA/
& ROARMAG.ORG/ESSAYS/OAXACA-TEACHER-STRIKE-POLICE-ATTACK/

p. 36–37. *image:* Police protect burned and looted CVS during Baltimore Uprising, April 27, 2015

p. 38–39. Harris County Sheriff Ron Hickman at press conference regarding the killing of Harris County officer Darren Goforth
YOUTUBE.COM/WATCH?V=ZFICPJ5CUA0

p. 40. Famous leaked interview with Lee Atwater, Republican Strategist, on the "Southern Strategy" using racial codes to appeal to southern whites, 1981
THENATION.COM/ARTICLE/EXCLUSIVE-LEE-ATWATERS-INFAMOUS-1981-INTERVIEW-SOUTHERN-STRATEGY/

p. 41. Justin Moore, "Small Town USA" lyrics, 2009
YOUTUBE.COM/WATCH?V=8VGEU_X17QU

p. 42. *image:* Lynyrd Skynyrd fashion t-shirt (male)

p. 43. *image:* Lynyrd Skynyrd fashion t-shirt (female)

p. 44–45. David Brookes, "Listening to Ta-Nehisi Coates While White," 2015
NYTIMES.COM/2015/07/17/OPINION/LISTENING-TO-TA-NEHISI-COATES-WHILE-WHITE.HTML

59

P. 44–45. Angela Davis interviewed from Prison in California in 1972, excerpted from *Black Power Mixtape*, 2011
YOUTUBE.COM/WATCH?V=2HNDONDVJVE

P. 46–47. *image:* CBS News story on Marissa Alexander with Hillary Clinton Presidential campaign ad, 2012/2016
CBSNEWS.COM/NEWS/FLA-WOMAN-MARISSA-ALEXANDER-GETS-20-YEARS-FOR-WARNING-SHOT-DID-SHE-STAND-HER-GROUND/

P. 48. *image:* Retailer sells confederate flag merch

P. 48–49. *image:* Tea Party rally with "Don't Tread on Me" flags, 2009

P. 50. Scott Walker speaks at the Iowa Freedom Summit, 2015
YOUTUBE.COM/WATCH?V=TMRA5XP_T10

P. 51. *image:* Farmer pulls down police barricade in Brussels outside EU headquarters, September 7, 2015
DAILYMAIL.CO.UK/NEWS/ARTICLE-3225155/THOUSANDS-DAIRY-FARMERS-SET-LIGHT-HAYSTACKS-SPRAY-POLICE-HAY-EGGS-FURIOUS-PROTESTS-OUTSIDE-EU-HEADQUARTERS-BRUSSELS-LOW-PRICE-PRODUCE.HTML

P. 52–53. Transcript from closing sequence in Haile Gerima's film *Bush Mama*, 1975

P. 52–53. Rally / press conference for the Campaign to Support Darren Wilson, April 23, 2014
YOUTUBE.COM/WATCH?V=4UCVN4IZNQC

P. 54–55. *image:* Police draw assault rifles on protesters in Ferguson to forcibly remove them from the business district, August 11, 2014

P. 56–57. Transcript from Peter Watkins' film *La Commune (Paris 1871)*, 2000